Orton Gillingham Materials

Workbook with 100 activities to improve writing and reading skills in children with dyslexia

Age: 7-8 years old

Shirley J. Woodhouse

Introduction

Teaching a child with dyslexia read: Dyslexia is a specific and persistent learning disability that affects reading and writing. For children with dyslexia, learning to read and write can be a difficult challenge for families and educators to tackle. For these children, written language becomes a great barrier, often without meaning or logic, which generates rejection of the task, frustration and discomfort.

The child with dyslexia is a child who has significant difficulties in reading and writing, because their brain processes information differently than other children; which is why if we expect the same results following the traditional method, we will find many barriers that can and often do harm the child. It is important to become aware of the characteristics of this difficulty, so as to help the child learn to read and the consequent overcoming of their difficulties such as understanding, knowledge and attention to their needs.

Reading difficulties with dyslexia

Dyslexia is a learning disability of neurobiological origin, which causes seem to be in the maturation and structuring of certain brain structures.

Dyslexia is therefore a condition of the brain which causes it to process information differently, making it difficult for the person to understand letters, their sounds, their combinations, etc.

Human language is a language based on signs, letters and their sounds, which are arbitrary. The correspondence of each grapheme (letter) with its phoneme (sound), does not follow any logic; it' simply chance. This is one of the greatest difficulties that children face when they have to learn to read and write. Converting the spoken language, they know into signs and transforming sounds into letters is a challenge.

This is even more complicated in children with dyslexia; the relationship becomes something indecipherable for them. No matter how hard they try, they cannot make sense of that dance between letters and sounds.

Children with dyslexia have a lot of difficulty recognizing letters; sometimes they mistake letters for others, write them backwards, etc.

Another difficulty they face, is knowing the sound that corresponds to each letter; and things get even more complicated when we combine several letters and we have to know several sounds.

New words are a challenge for them and they can forget them easily, so they must work hard to acquire them. Sometimes they read certain words effortlessly, but the next day they completely forget them.

When they write, they omit letters, change their position, forget words in a sentence, etc.

Dyslexia also affects reading comprehension. When they read, they are trying really hard to decipher and understand each word, sometimes even each letter; that is why the meaning of the text gets lost.

Reading comprehension: Activities to help develop it in children

How to teach a child with dyslexia to read

A child with dyslexia has difficulty learning to read and write, because it is hard for them to recognize letters and to know which sound they correspond to. However, the child can learn to read and write and overcome those difficulties. Remember that dyslexia is a learning difficulty that does not imply any physical or mental handicap; the child with dyslexia has adequate capacities. In order to teach a child with dyslexia to read, it is essential to know the natur their difficulties, understand them and use a teaching method that responds to their needs.

A child with dyslexia

A teaching method to help a child with dyslexia read

In the first place, it is necessary to make an assessment of the child, to know their reading and writing level, the nature and characteristics of their difficulties in order to understand their specific needs. For this, it is advisable to seek a specialist.

It favors the development of phonological awareness (which consists of the correspondence of the sound with the letter). To do this, start with simple activities, letter by letter. Even if other children around the same age read full texts, it may be necessary to start working letter by letter. Later, we can continue with the words, phrases and texts. It is about dedicating more time and more detail to the learning process.

Phonological awareness worksheets

Use motivational activities that are engaging. Do not limit the child to just paper and pencil: they can make letters out of play dough, write on sand with their fingers, play catch or games such as hangman, word searches, crossword puzzles, etc.

Don't force them to read or read a lot. Try to have them read on a daily basis, little by little; sometimes a sentence or a paragraph is enough. Help them understand what they read, ask them questions, ask them to read again, etc.

Table of Contents

Identify and circle the words beginning with 'b' using the red color pencil and circle the words beginning with 'd' using the blue color pencil.

(base)   (data)   doll   back

drum   ball   bat   deck   belt

deal   bill   dark   bell   dab

begin   bark   dial   best   blame

bless   disk   beak   brown   dress

break   draw   brisk   dear   bear

Write five words beginning with 'b' and 'd'.

_____   _____

_____   _____

_____   _____

_____   _____

pay   queen   quirk   parade

pick   quilt   paste   quick   quiet

pain   pale   park   quail   quit

question   paint   party   quest

quarter   play   quack   poison

pick   quill   pray   quote   press

Write five words beginning with 'p' and 'q'.

_____   _____

_____   _____

_____   _____

_____   _____

_____   _____

2

Identify and circle the words beginning with 'm' using the red color pencil and circle the words beginning with 'w' using the blue color pencil.

(met)   (wet)   mass   wear

make   water   wait   mess   whale

master   we   me   mam   wall

wire   man   went   mail   male

what   married   waste   waist

mango   watch   main   wake   mat

Write five words beginning with 'm' and 'w'.

_____   _____

_____   _____

_____   _____

_____   _____

_____   _____

(net) (up) under neat

nest under nail nest urchin

new use next umbrella

urgent nurse nap utensils

newt urge null urge

news unhappy nil unique

Write five words beginning with 'n' and 'u'.

_____ _____

_____ _____

_____ _____

_____ _____

_____ _____

ink   jet   insect   jug

jaguar   in   jail   it   judge

ill   jar   jacket   igloo

jelly   indigo   just   ice

isle   jam   just   insist

jewelry   iguana   jumbo   jet

Write five words beginning with 'i' and 'j'.

_____   _____

_____   _____

_____   _____

_____   _____

_____   _____

fat   team   fair   test

team   fit   tiger   tell   fan

feel   tear   frog   true

fat   tell   fair   try

take   fear   trust   trick

tail   fast   fail   fuel

Write five words bnbeginning with 'f' and 't'.

_____   _____

_____   _____

_____   _____

_____   _____

_____   _____

Solve the jumbled word puzzles and match
the words with the correct picture.

maelc

erde

woc

tlepaneh

eorsh

odg

tac

rofg

iursrelq

ilno

ukcd

glaf

riworferks

sipoclep

rumd

keroct

ipe

lilrg

tah

obx

nva

bltea

8

Solve the jumbled word puzzles and match the words with the correct picture.

hsoeu

rfmea

edb

tse

lobkcs

plaotp

omcptuer

okbo

oard

ecsht

ebortrh

Solve the jumbled word puzzles and match the words with the correct picture.

onaerepeal

siph

rca

kieb

rtcuk

cyaht

ubs

artni

toba

trac

bca

Rearrange the jumbled sentences.

dog The running is

_____

are Who you

_____

is biggest the mammal Elephant The

_____

taking is Cat nap a The

_____

loves with her play sister She to

_____

arrived He to late birthday the party

_____

dancing loves She

_____

Rearrange the jumbled sentences.

dog catches stick The the

_____

cat to park the walked The

_____

a student chair sat The on.

_____

The reads story teacher students the to a

_____

fat The cat was

_____

toys Please, away your put

_____

lamp on turned the Mom

_____

Rearrange the jumbled sentences.

like pigs roll to mud the in The

_____

new have I bike a

_____

chocolate you cream do ice like

_____

baby took the nap a sleepy

_____

am old eight I years

_____

wearing her a hair is ribbon blue she in

_____

about a book Jack animals read

_____

Rearrange the jumbled sentences.

around cars track The raced

_____

won team Sarah's game the soccer

_____

like summer to you in swimming Do the go

_____

under the Fish sea live

_____

a hat new got has Sam

_____

playing the It is fun snow in

_____

is car Our blue

_____

Rearrange the jumbled sentences.

The is in the tree ball

_____

leaves falling are to the ground The orange

_____

Is a tall oak tree This

_____

I to play baseball in the park like

_____

Don't We like jog to

_____

On Sam is going swimming Wednesday

_____

We went by bike the park on Sunday to

_____

Combine the two sentences using the correct conjunction in brackets.

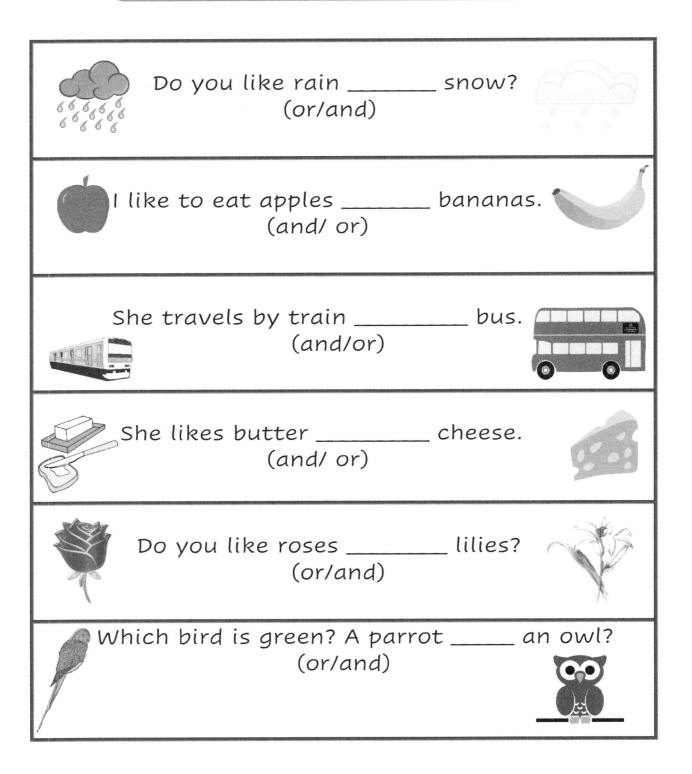

Do you like rain _____ snow?
(or/and)

I like to eat apples _____ bananas.
(and/ or)

She travels by train _____ bus.
(and/or)

She likes butter _____ cheese.
(and/ or)

Do you like roses _____ lilies?
(or/and)

Which bird is green? A parrot _____ an owl?
(or/and)

Combine the two sentences using the correct conjunction in brackets. Write 'and' / 'or'.

Nathan likes chocolate.

_____

He likes ice cream.

The girls went to the mall.

_____

They went to the store.

Mother asked us to clean our room.

_____

She asked us to vacuum.

Do you want salad with your meat?

_____

Do you want rice?

Put the cheese in the tin.

_____

Cover it with the lid.

You can eat either orange.

_____

Banana.

Combine the two sentences using the correct conjunction in brackets. Write 'and' / 'but'.

My grandma makes tasty food	_____	snacks.
Her writing is very good,	_____	her reading is not so good.
Marco	_____	Carlos are playing outside.
I am not a very good runner,	_____	I always do my best.
I want to see a movie	_____	eat popcorn.
She has a blue	_____	a red color.

| Jim is not polite | _____ | no one likes him. |

| Dan did not study for the quiz | _____ | he did not score the full marks. |

| I am hungry | _____ | I did not have my breakfast. |

| The kitchen is dirty | _____ | You did not clean it. |

| There are good books in the library | _____ | you can read there. |

| I asked him to come | _____ | he came |

Combine the two sentences using the correct conjunction in brackets.

| It is cold, | _____ | I wear my hat and muffler. |

| I want cake, | _____ | I am not allowed. |

| I would go, | _____ | it is too far. |

| I will finish my homework, | _____ | then I can play video games. |

| John got dressed, | _____ | he forgot his socks! |

| The teacher is talking, | _____ | we need to listen. |

Underline the adverb in each sentence.

The dog cheerfully jumped around the house.

My teacher patiently waited for our class to finish our quiz.

Helen kindly offered to her mother.

My sister happily played outside.

Jack silently finished his meal.

David finished the homework quickly.

I finished reading the book quietly.

The bunny magically appeared out of the hat.

that	the	not	on
the	sit	as	hate
as	the	to	the

_____

- -

_____

four	four	but	four
as	sit	four	hate
by	four	bit	four

_____

- -

_____

'The'

Write the word in the blank boxes.

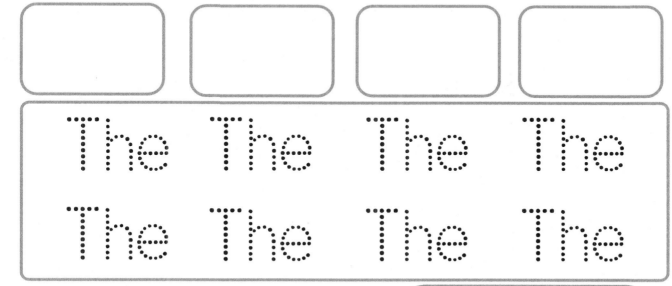

The The The The

The The The The

Connect the words 'the' by drawing a line.

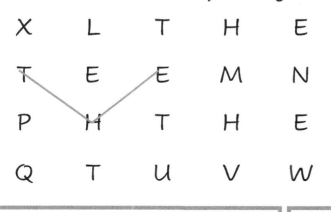

X	L	T	H	E
T	E	E	M	N
P	H	T	H	E
Q	T	U	V	W

Find the words 'the'.

t	a	c	f	r	k	l
h	l	t	h	e	m	r
e	q	w	s	l	m	n
u	r	t	h	e	n	h
o	u	s	e	m	n	o

Underline the word 'the'.

The black cat is very naughty.

The sun shines bright.

The moon is beautiful.

He saw the queen.

She wrote a letter to the mayor.

Fill in the blank spaces.

_____ black cat is very naughty

_____sun shines bright.

_____ moon is beautiful.

He saw _____queen.

She wrote a letter to _____mayor.

'four'

Write the word in the blank boxes.

four four four four

four four four four

Connect the words 'four' by drawing a line.

X	F	T	H	F
F	O	U	R	O
P	U	T	H	U
Q	R	U	V	R

Find the words 'four'.

t	a	c	f	r	f	l
r	f	t	x	e	o	r
u	q	o	s	l	u	n
o	r	t	u	e	r	h
f	u	s	e	r	n	o

Circle the word 'four'.

I saw four birds on the tree.

My brother is four years old.

My mother has four siblings.

We went to the park at four PM.

I ate four cookies.

Fill in the blank spaces.

I saw _____birds on the tree.

My brother is _____ years old.

My mother has _____ siblings.

We went to the park at _____ PM.

I ate _____ cookies.

Color the word 'once'. Write a sentence using the word 'once'.

oak	once	or	once
once	oil	once	off
of	offer	once	once

_____

_____

Color the word 'two'. Write a sentence using the word 'two'.

for	two	she	two
two	here	two	him
two	all	bit	two

_____

_____

'once'

Write the word in the blank boxes.

[ ] [ ] [ ] [ ]

once once once once

once once once once

Connect the words 'once' by drawing a line.

X   F   T   E   O

O   N   C   E   N

P   N   T   H   C

O   R   U   V   E

Find the words 'once'.

t a c f r f l

o n c e e o r

u q o s l n n

o n c e e c h

f o n c e e o

Circle the word 'once'.

Once upon a time, there lived a beautiful girl. She met the prince only once in her life. The girl once worked in the castle. She was once a cook in the castle. She once owned a furry cat. She is a nice girl once you get to know her.

Answer the following questions.

What is the passage about?

_____

_____

Where did the girl work?

_____

_____

'two'

Write the word in the blank boxes.

☐ ☐ ☐ ☐

two two two two

two two two two

Connect the words 'two' by drawing a line.

T	F	O	E	T
O	W	C	E	W
T	N	O	H	O
O	T	W	O	E

Find the words 'two'.

t	a	c	t	r	f	l
w	n	t	w	o	o	r
o	q	o	o	l	n	n
t	w	o	e	x	c	h
f	t	w	o	x	e	o

Circle the word 'two'.

There were two loving siblings who used to adopt kids. They had adopted two children already. They were thinking about adopting two more children. They had two kittens in the house. They also had two cute dogs. They called their two adopted children and asked them if they were ok with two

Answer the following questions.

Who adopted the children?

_____

How many children were living in the house?

_____

How many kittens were in the house?

_____

How many dogs were in the house?

_____

27

Color the word 'too'. Write a sentence using the word 'too'.

is	too	not	on
too	sit	too	will
too	too	to	there

Color the word 'of'. Write a sentence using the word 'of'.

all	of	but	of
as	of	of	hate
of	well	bit	of

'too'

Write the word in the blank boxes.

too too too too

too too too too

Connect the words 'too' by drawing a line.

Y	F	O	E	T
I	O	C	E	O
T	N	T	O	O
O	T	T	O	O

Find the words 'too'.

t	a	c	t	r	f	l
o	n	t	o	o	l	r
o	t	o	o	k	n	n
t	o	o	e	x	c	h
f	t	o	o	x	e	o

Circle the word 'too'.

It was too cold outside. He wore his leather jacket. He felt too warm in that one. It was not too late to change his mind as he had so many jackets in his closet. So, he wore another jacket which was not too warm for him.

Answer the following questions.

How was the weather outside?

_____

What did the boy wear?

_____

Fill in the blanks

He felt _____ warm in that one.

It was not _____ late to change his mind.

It was _____ cold outside.

29

'of'

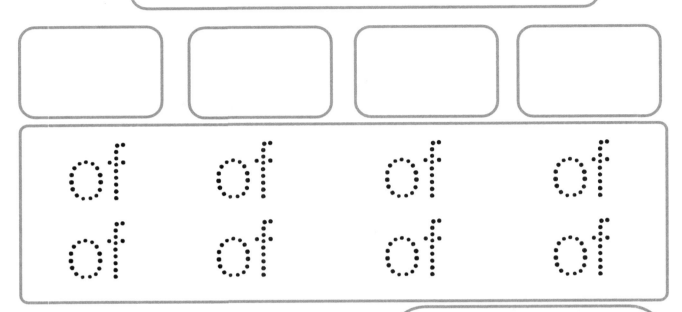

Connect the words 'of' by drawing a line.

O	F	O	E	T
I	O	F	E	O
T	F	T	F	F
O	T	T	O	O

Find the words 'of'.

t	a	o	f	r	f	o
j	n	t	o	f	l	f
o	t	o	f	k	n	n
f	l	o	p	f	c	h
f	o	f	o	m	e	o

Circle the word 'of'.

The houses of the city were all made of glass. Ethen wanted one of his own. All three of Ethen's brothers had beautiful houses. Certainly, he had been under a lot of social pressure to have his own house.

Answer the following questions.

What were the houses of the city made up of?

_____

_____

_____

Fill in the blanks

_____ wanted one of his own.

The houses of the city were all

_____ .

Color the word 'for'. Write a sentence using the word 'for'.

for	to	not	hair
for	sit	for	hence
him	her	hand	for

_____

_____

Color the word 'how'. Write a sentence using the word 'how'.

what	how	how	wind
how	when	wink	well
where	how	whose	how

_____

_____

'for'

for for   for   for

for for   for   for

Connect the words 'for' by drawing a line.

O	F	O	R	T
I	O	F	O	K
T	O	O	F	Y
R	T	R	S	M

Find the words 'for'.

t	a	o	f	o	r	o
f	n	t	o	f	f	f
o	t	f	o	r	o	n
r	f	o	r	f	r	h
f	o	f	o	r	e	o

Circle the word 'for'.

Alexa bought beautiful clothes for the trip. She had been waiting for this trip for nearly a year. She waited for her friends to reach home. They all waited for the train at the station for five hours.

Answer the following questions.

What is the name of the girl?

_____

What did Alexa buy for the trip?

_____

How long has she been waiting for this trip?

_____

_____

32

'how'

[ ] [ ] [ ] [ ]

how how how how
how how how how

Connect the words 'how' by drawing a line.

H	O	W	R	H
O	O	W	H	O
W	O	O	O	W
H	T	R	W	M

Find the words 'how'.

h	a	o	f	o	r	o
o	n	t	o	h	o	w
w	t	h	o	w	o	n
r	h	o	w	f	r	h
f	o	h	o	w	e	o

Circle the word 'how'.

No matter how sorry Alex was for what had happened, or how many times he had apologized, he couldn't remove the hurt. How could he remove the pain he caused? How could he make it up to his friend?

Answer the following questions.

What is the name of the boy?

_____

How did he feel about the situation?

_____

_____

_____

_____

33

Color the word 'by'. Write a sentence using the word 'by'.

that	this	them	by
by	sit	then	thin
think	by	by	thus

_____

- -

_____

Color the word 'put'. Write a sentence using the word 'put'.

he	put	him	put
put	hair	put	hint
hen	put	head	put

_____

- -

_____

'by'

Write the word in the blank boxes.

by by by by
by by by by

Connect the words 'by' by drawing a line.

H	B	Y	R	B
B	O	W	H	Y
Y	O	B	Y	Y
H	T	R	B	M

Find the words 'by'.

b	a	o	b	y	r	b
y	n	t	o	h	b	y
w	t	b	y	w	y	n
r	h	o	w	f	r	h
f	o	b	y	w	e	o

Circle the word 'by'.

He was stunned by my beauty. I have been blessed by nature to have such a pretty face. By the time I reached the teen age, I had turned into a beautiful girl. I thought that by the age of thirty, I would no longer be beautiful.

Fill in the blanks.

He was _____ by my beauty.

I have been blessed _____nature to have such a _____ face.

_____the time I _____the teen age, I had turned into a beautiful girl.

I thought that _____ the age of thirty, I would no longer be _____.

35

'put'

Write the word in the blank boxes.

put put put put

put put put put

Connect the words 'put' by drawing a line.

P	U	T	R	P
U	O	W	P	U
T	O	B	U	T
P	U	T	T	M

Find the words 'put'.

p	u	t	b	y	r	p
y	n	t	o	h	b	u
w	t	p	u	t	y	t
r	h	o	w	f	r	h
p	u	t	y	w	e	o

Underline the words 'put'.

She put on her red dress.

Mother put aside the clothes.

He put a spoon in her hand.

The dog was put to sleep.

He put the birds in the cage.

Fill in the blanks.

She _____ on her _____ dress.

Mother _____ aside the _____.

He _____ a _____ in her hand.

The _____ was _____ to sleep.

He _____ the birds in the _____.

U V W X Y Z A B C D E F G H I J K

Color the word 'does'. Write a sentence using the word 'does'.

does	does	be	does
does	being	does	bell
bit	does	braid	does

Color the word 'whose'. Write a sentence using the word 'whose'.

whose	what	whose	where
whose	who	when	whom
where	what	whose	whose

'does'

Write the word in the blank boxes.

does   does   does   does

does   does   does   does

Connect the words 'does' by drawing a line.

D   O   E   S   S

O   V   M   E   U

E   D   O   U   T

S   D   O   E   S

Find the words 'does'.

d	b	e	d	y	r	p
y	n	d	o	e	s	f
w	t	p	e	t	y	t
d	o	e	s	f	r	h
p	u	t	y	w	e	o

Underline the words 'does'.

He does not like to do anything else.

Why does the rain fall?

What difference does it make?

Does human activity cause the planet to warm?

He does not want my help.

Fill in the blanks.

He _____ not like to do anything else.

Why _____ the _____ fall?

What difference _____ it make?

_____ human activity cause the _____ to warm?

He _____ not want my help.

'whose'

Write the word in the blank boxes.

[ ] [ ] [ ] [ ]

whose whose whose whose

whose whose whose whose

Connect the words 'whose' by drawing a line.

W H O S E
O V M E U
W H O S E
S D O E S

Find the words 'whose'.

w h o s e r w
y n d o e s h
w h o s e y o
d o e s f r s
p u t y w e e

Underline the words 'whose'.

1. Whose child is it? They asked him.

2. And whose sheep are these?

3. I buy my eggs from a farmer whose chickens roam free.

4. But the fourth lawyer, whose name was Abraham Lincoln, stopped.

5. He did not know whose it was; it belonged to the pond.

Make five sentences using the word 'whose'.

_____

_____

_____

_____

_____

_____

wear	wed	wind	wire
will	wear	wheel	wear
wear	west	wear	wear

Color the word 'woman'. Write a sentence using the word 'woman.

woman	when	where	what
who	woman	which	woman
where	wheel	woman	whale

'wear'

wear wear wear wear

wear wear wear wear

Connect the words 'wear' by drawing a line.

W	E	A	R	R
O	V	A	E	A
L	E	O	S	E
W	R	A	E	W

Find the words 'wear'.

w	e	a	r	e	r	w
y	n	d	r	e	s	e
w	e	a	r	e	y	a
d	e	e	s	f	r	r
w	u	t	y	w	e	e

Underline the words 'wear'.

1. You'd better wear a coat.
2. What would you have me wear, a sweat suit?
3. At present men make shift to wear what they can get.
4. "Did you not wear green whiskers at one time?" he asked.
5. You're going to wear it out just looking at it.

Make five sentences using the word 'wear'.

_____

_____

_____

_____

_____

_____

41

'woman' | Write the word in the blank boxes.

woman woman woman

woman woman woman

Connect the words 'wear' by drawing a line.

N	A	M	O	W
O	V	A	E	A
W	O	M	A	N
W	R	S	E	W

Find the words 'woman'.

w	o	m	a	n	r	w
y	n	d	a	e	s	e
w	e	m	r	e	y	a
d	o	e	s	f	r	r
w	u	t	y	w	e	e

Underline the words 'woman'.

1. You are the most beautiful woman I have ever seen.

2. A woman was sitting alone by the fire.

3. She's a woman one could easily fall in love with.

4. The woman laughed softly.

5. "You!" cried the woman in great surprise.

Make five sentences using the word 'woman'.

_____

_____

_____

_____

_____

_____

Color the word 'build'. Write a
sentence using the word 'build'.

build	beer	bed	build
build	bear	build	best
base	build	bar	back

_____

Color the word 'half'. Write a
sentence using the word 'half'.

half	heart	half	hard
hat	half	his	hail
half	him	hen	half

_____

'build' | Write the word in the blank boxes.

build   build   build   build

build   build   build   build

Connect the words 'BUILD' by drawing a line.

B   U   I   L   D

O   V   A   E   A

B   U   I   L   D

W   R   S   E   W

Find the words 'build'.

b	u	i	l	d	d	w
y	n	d	a	l	s	e
w	d	l	i	u	b	a
d	o	u	s	f	r	r
w	b	t	y	w	e	e

Underline the words 'build'.

1. He paused, to build the suspense.

2. Alex decided to build a room upstairs for his office.

3. They could build on that.

4. Birds build their nests in the trees.

5. I will build a house for her.

Make five sentences using the word 'build'.

_____

_____

_____

_____

_____

_____

'half' | Write the word in the blank boxes.

[ ] [ ] [ ] [ ]

half half half half half

half half half half half

Connect the words 'half' by drawing a line.

H	A	L	F	H
O	V	L	E	A
B	A	l	L	L
H	R	S	E	F

Find the words 'half'.

b	u	i	f	d	d	w
y	n	l	a	f	s	e
w	a	l	i	l	b	a
h	a	l	f	a	r	r
w	b	t	y	h	e	e

Underline the words 'half'.

1. I was awake half the night.

2. I arrived half an hour late to the party.

3. I was halfway through my assignment.

4. And that was almost half a century ago!

5. I gave her half of my sandwich.

Make five sentences using the word 'half'.

_____

_____

_____

_____

_____

_____

Color the word 'dye'. Write a sentence using the word 'dye'.

dog	do	dot	dye
dye	drum	dial	dye
drink	dye	dam	doll

_____

- -

_____

Color the word 'also'. Write a sentence using the word 'also'.

also	air	ask	also
apple	hair	aunt	aid
also	her	also	arm

_____

- -

_____

'dye'   Write the word in the blank boxes.

dye   dye   dye   dye   dye

dye   dye   dye   dye   dye

Connect the words 'dye' by drawing a line.

D   Y   E   F   D

O   V   L   Y   A

D   Y   E   L   L

H   D   Y   E   F

Find the words 'dye'.

d	y	e	f	d	d	w
y	n	y	a	d	s	e
w	a	d	d	y	e	a
h	a	l	f	e	r	r
w	d	y	e	h	v	e

Underline the words 'dye'.

1. she had to dye her hair black.

2. He put blue dye on his shirt.

3. The dye did not work on her bag.

4. She used fresh leaves to obtain a green colored dye.

Make five sentences using the word 'dye'.

_____

_____

_____

_____

_____

_____

V W X Y Z A B C D E F G H I J K L

'also'

Write the word in the blank boxes.

also also also also also

also also also also also

Connect the words 'also' by drawing a line.

D	G	E	O	A
O	V	S	Y	L
A	L	S	O	S
A	D	Y	E	O

Find the words 'also'.

a	l	s	o	d	a	w
l	n	y	a	d	l	e
s	a	l	s	o	s	a
o	s	l	a	e	o	r
w	d	y	e	h	v	e

Underline the words 'also'.

1. Also my hat is quite empty.

2. He was also concerned about his neighbors.

3. Both Sam and Nick would also attend the party.

4. The danger had also passed.

5. She also lost her sense of taste.

Make five sentences using the word 'also'.

_____

_____

_____

_____

_____

_____

Color the word 'great'. Write a sentence using the word 'great'.

giant	great	gum	grow
great	guest	gate	great
glide	great	gig	green

_____

- -

_____

Color the word 'gone'. Write a sentence using the word 'gone'.

ghost	gone	grow	gone
gone	goal	gone	grapes
get	gone	got	gone

_____

- -

_____

'great'

great   great   great   great

great   great   great   great

Connect the words 'great' by drawing a line.

G	R	E	A	T
O	V	S	Y	L
G	R	E	A	T
A	D	Y	E	O

Find the words 'great'.

g	r	e	a	t	a	g
l	r	y	a	d	l	r
s	a	e	s	o	s	e
g	r	e	a	t	o	a
w	d	y	e	t	v	t

Underline the words 'great'.

1.My great grandfather served in armed forces.

2. Cindy did a great job.

3. She said, "it's great and I love it."

4. There is a great view up here.

5. He was the first great American poet.

Make five sentences using the word 'great'.

_____

_____

_____

_____

_____

_____

'gone' | Write the word in the blank boxes.

gone   gone   gone   gone

gone   gone   gone   gone

Connect the words 'gone' by drawing a line.

G   O   N   E   E

O   V   N   Y   N

G   O   E   A   O

G   D   Y   E   G

Find the words 'gone'.

g   o   n   e   t   a   g

l   r   y   a   d   l   o

s   g   o   n   e   s   n

g   r   e   a   t   o   e

g   o   n   e   t   v   t

Underline the words 'gone'.

1. Linda would be gone for two days.

2. The farm boy has gone to the city.

3. With everyone gone she could enjoy herself.

4. This fight had gone too far.

5. He must have gone straight to the house.

Make five sentences using the word 'gone'.

_____

_____

_____

_____

_____

_____

Draw a line to complete the word and match it with the correct picture.

cl   ip

cl   ay

cl   own

cl   aw

cl   iff

cl   ap

cl   ock

cl   oud

Make words using the initial blend "cl" and fill in the blank spaces with the correct word.

cl		There is a _____ at the birthday party.
cl		It was 8' O _____ when I reached home.
cl		Children were making hand prints on the _____.
cl		A group of students were _____ing and singing songs.
cl		Rainy _____ are in the sky.
cl		Can you place this paper _____ on the table?
cl		She never saw such a rocky _____ in her life.
cl		I am afraid of eagles' _____.

V W X Y Z A B C D E F G H I J K L

Cleo is late for her class. She did not watch the clock. She was busy in the clinic. Cleo has changed her clothes. As her clothes were not clean. She kept an extra dress in the closet to change in the clinic. She closed the door and changed clothes. She hurried to class.

pl	ay
pl	anet
pl	ug
pl	ate
pl	um
pl	ane
pl	ank
pl	ant

55

Make words using the initial blend "pl" and fill in the blank spaces with the correct word.

pl		He likes to _____ in the park.
pl		My mother likes to _____ vegetables in our home garden.
pl		I bought a _____ for my younger brother.
pl		Insert the _____ into the socket.
pl		Sarah was eating _____.
pl		I ordered two _____ of rice.
pl		The name of our _____ is earth.
pl		I saw a wooden _____ floating in the water.

Platt liked to learn about planets. His favorite planet was Pluto. He named his pet dog after his favorite planet Pluto. He plays with Pluto all day long. People say Pluto is not a planet anymore! Platt was sad about Pluto, the planet. His favorite plate has the pictures of all the planets on it. From all the places he visited recently he liked the museum so far.

Draw a line to complete the word and match it with the correct picture.

gl	ass
gl	asses
gl	obe
gl	ad
gl	ue
gl	ove
gl	ow
gl	ide

Make words using the initial blend "gl"
and fill in the blank spaces with the
correct word.

gl		Ethen is trying hard to find his country on the _____.
gl		Sid was _____ to see me.
gl		Can you fetch a _____ of water?
gl		My grandfather's _____ are broken and he cannot see properly.
gl		The bride's skin was _____ing with happiness.
gl		I tried to paste the buttons with a _____.
gl		Her hands were freezing so I gave her my _____.
gl		The plane managed to _____ down the runway.

Gloria likes things that gleam, glitter and glow. She was glad to see her new glowing bracelet. She likes glittering glaciers. She likes glowing gems and she also likes gleaming glass. Gloria is full of glee. She is not gloomy.

Draw a line to complete the word and match it with the correct picture.

bl	ue	
bl	ack	
bl	ade	
bl	ender	
bl	ocks	
bl	anket	
bl	oom	
bl	ood	

Make words using the initial blend "bl"
and fill in the blank spaces with the
correct word.

bl		Nick's favorite color is _____.
bl		My mother knitted a _____ for my cat.
bl		Ocean seems _____ in color.
bl		The flowers _____ in spring.
bl		Sam's father was making juice in the _____.
bl		I make big buildings with _____.
bl		Be careful the _____ is sharp.
bl		My brother often donates _____.

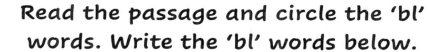

Blake likes to play with blocks. He likes blue blocks. He also likes black blocks. He has ten blue blocks. He lost one blue block and was blank where he kept it? Blake blamed Blane that he took his blue block. "I did not take your blue block, Blane blurted with anger. Blake found his blue block hidden under the black blanket. Blake blushed and apologized to Blane.

Draw a line to complete the word and match it with the correct picture.

fl	ower	
fl	y	
fl	ask	
fl	ag	
fl	ock	
fl	oor	
fl	oat	
fl	amingo	

U V W X Y Z A B C D E F G H I J K L

Make words using the initial blend "fl"
and fill in the blank spaces with the
correct word.

fl		The Plane _____ high in the air.
fl		The ship _____ in deep ocean.
fl		The _____ is a beautiful bird.
fl		_____ bloom in spring.
fl		I saw a _____ of geese.
fl		Walk carefully the _____ is wet.
fl		I was marching with the _____ on Independence Day.
fl		Put the _____ down you may break it.

Flan the flamingo is from Florida. Flan the flamingo likes to play flute. Flan the flamingo flips the pancakes. Flan the flamingo likes flowers and flip flops. Flan the flamingo likes to fly high. Flan the flamingo likes to float in water. Flan the flamingo dances on the floor. Flan the flamingo doesn't like to live with its flock.

66

Draw a line to complete the word and match it with the correct picture.

br	ick	
br	own	
br	ead	
br	anch	
br	ain	
br	ide	
br	oom	
br	ush	

Make words using the initial blend "br" and fill in the blank spaces with the correct word.

br		The boy was making a _____ wall.
br		Doctor recommended me a _____ scan.
br		She was a beautiful _____ .
br		I ate _____ with butter for breakfast.
br		She was _____ing her hair.
br		Mother asked me to bring the _____ to clean the floor.
br		The birds were sitting on the _____.
br		She bought a _____ jacket.

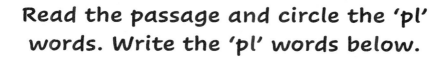

Brad's mom made breakfast for him. She broke an egg and made an omelet. Brad took bread and ate it with the omelet. Brad likes bread very much. He eats bread for breakfast, brunch and dinner. Brad and his little sister Brianna sweep their rooms with the broom. They always brush their teeth before going to bed. Brad told Brianna a story about a beautiful bride before going to sleep.

st	ick	
st	amp	
st	and	
st	ove	
st	one	
st	ore	
st	op	
st	ar	

76

Make words using the initial blend "st" and fill in the blank spaces with the correct word.

st		The teacher made us _____ by the wall as a punishment.
st		I have pasted the _____ on the letter.
st		The dog was playing with a _____.
st		My aunt bakes cookies on the _____.
st		I had to _____ at the red signal.
st		Last night I saw so many _____ in the sky.
st		Sam brought eggs and bread from the grocery _____.
st		Sarah was throwing _____ in the pond.

Stephen has a dog named Steve. Steve never stops playing with a stick. Stephen's room is upstairs. Stephen loves watching stars at night. Steve stays up with Stephen till he falls asleep. Steve waits for Stephen to get up in the morning, standing beside his bed.

tr	ap	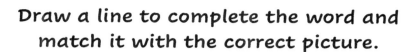
tr	ain	
tr	ash	
tr	umpet	
tr	ack	
tr	trunk	
tr	ee	
tr	uck	 

V W X Y Z A B C D E F G H I J K L

Make words using the initial blend; "tr" and fill in the blank spaces with the correct word.

tr		Sarah's father drives a _____.
tr		The _____ makes the choo choo sound.
tr		I saw apples on the _____.
tr		There were four cars racing on the _____.
tr		I threw the _____ in the bin.
tr		I set a _____ for the rat.
tr		She plays _____ in the band.
tr		I saw an old tree's _____ in the park.

U V W X Y Z A B C D E F G H I J K

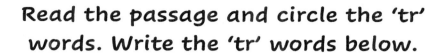

Tracy is trusted by everyone. Tracy always tells the truth. She treats people nicely. Tracy stays away from trouble. She is a true friend of nature. She loves trees and flowers. She travels by train to see the beauty of the world. Her trips are often planned with her family.

Draw a line to complete the word and match it with the correct picture.

cr	y
cr	ack
cr	ib
cr	ayon
cr	ab
cr	ane
cr	oss
cr	own

Make words using the initial blend; "cr" and fill in the blank spaces with the correct word.

cr		Linda fell down and started _____.
cr		To make an omelet you have to _____ an egg.
cr		My mother always wears a _____ pendent.
cr		I saw a _____ crawling on the sea shore.
cr		She like using _____ to color.
cr		My mother wore a beautiful _____ at her wedding.
cr		The _____ was lifting heavy rocks.
cr		The baby was sleeping peacefully in the _____.

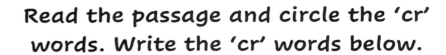

Read the passage and circle the 'cr' words. Write the 'cr' words below.

Crabby the crab crawls on the seashore. Crabby the crab likes to play with crocs. Crabby the crab does not let anyone cross his path. Crabby the crab is afraid of big cranes; he starts crying when he sees a big crane. Crabby the crab likes crayon colors and gold crowns.

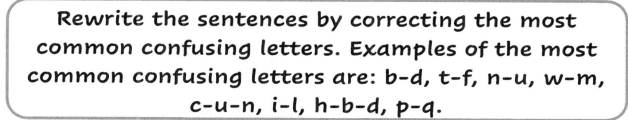

Rewrite the sentences by correcting the most common confusing letters. Examples of the most common confusing letters are: b–d, t–f, n–u, w–m, c–u–n, i–l, h–b–d, p–q.

Oue fine Snuday morning, Sawautha aud her frieuds mere playing on fhe deach.

_____

_____

Sawanfha mas wakiug a saub uasfle.

_____

Phoede mas collectiug sea sbells.

_____

Tla was fakiug a uap nuder an umdrella.

_____

Tiua mas smiwwing iu fhe sea.

_____

Tbey hab a deach sef fo qlay.

_____

Tbey all had tun.

_____

Rewrite the sentences by correcting the most common confusing letters. Examples of the most common confusing letters are: b-d, t-f, n-u, w-m, c-u-n, i-l, h-b-d, p-q, v-y.

The doats are tloatiug along the lakeshore.

_____

If is the snmwer doat parade.

_____

There are motor doats, rowpoats anb saildoats.

_____

Jessica's fayorite is fhe vellom wotor doat wifh the tlag.

_____

The rowdoaf becorated wifh flowers is Lisa's fayorite.

_____

Touy likes the qurqle saildoaf.

_____

The doats tloaf one af a fime.

_____

Sarab is my dest triend.

_____

She likes to eaf chocolafes.

_____

Me are in fhe same scbool.

_____

Her tavorite sudject is Wath.

_____

But I bo not like math.

_____

If is her dirthbay fobay.

_____

I bave dought a deautitul qurqle bress for ber.

_____

She looks very pretty.

_____

Sarah is my best friend. She likes to eat chocolates. We are in the same school. Her favorite subject is Math. But I do not like math. It is her birthday today. I have bought a beautiful purple dress for her. She looks very pretty. Her eyes are hazel and her hair is black, soft and long.

Rewrite the correct statements.

Samantha is my best friend.

_____

She likes to eat ice-cream.

_____

Her favorite subject is science.

_____

I have bought a beautiful bouquet for her.

_____

Her eyes are blue.

_____

She looks very elegant.

_____

Reading comprehension

The boats are floating along the lakeshore. It is the summer boat parade. There are motor boats, rowboats and sailboats. Jessica's favorite is the yellow motor boat with the flag. The rowboat decorated with flowers is Lisa's favorite. Tony likes the purple sailboat. The boats float one at a time. The people on the boats wave at the crowds. The crowds cheer the boats. The boat parade is really fun to watch. It is the best part of the summer.

Rewrite the correct statements.

The boats are floating along the seashore.

_____

It is the winter boat parade.

_____

There are motor bikes, rowboats and yachts.

_____

The rowboat decorated with flags is Lisa's favorite.

_____

The people on the boats smile at the crowds.

_____

Write 'a' or 'an' in the blank.

Articles   **'a'**   **or**   **'an'**

1. _____ flower and _____ butterfly.

2. _____ bus and _____ kite.

3. _____ pencil and _____ star.

4. _____ eye and _____ hand.

5. _____ fish and _____ starfish.

6. _____ man and _____ violin.

7. _____ apple and _____ cupcake.

8. _____ clown and _____ balloon.

9. _____ tree and _____ frog.

10. _____ hive and _____ bee.

Circle the correct article (a/an/the) in each sentence.

Articles   'a'   'an'   'the'

John wanted to read *a / an* comic book.

The class went on *a / an* field trip.

He likes to read *an / the / a* short story.

Lisa put *a / an / the* orange on her yogurt.

My mom likes to bake *a / the / an* cake.

The dog caught *a / an* stick.

I saw *a / an* otter at the zoo.

A / an / the oval is shaped like *a / an* egg.

A / An / The dog caught *a / an/ the* stick.

I quickly ate *a / an / the* cookies.

Write 'a', 'an' or 'the' in the blank.

Articles   'a'   'an'   'the'

I bought _____ orange bag for my little brother.

Coco is _____ lazy dog.

I am thirsty. Please give me _____ a glass of water.

She can ride _____ bike.

Vicky was dressed as _____ elf yesterday.

Every day I eat _____ egg for breakfast.

_____ tooth fairy came and took away my broken tooth.

There is _____ insect under the table.

Raechell was happy to get _____ gift from her parents.

_____ snail is faster than _____ caterpillar.

cl	ip	
cl	ay	
cl	own	
cl	aw	
cl	iff	
cl	ap	
cl	ock	
cl	oud	

This page is intentionally left blank.

pl	ay	
pl	anet	
pl	ug	
pl	ate	
pl	um	
pl	ane	
pl	ank	
pl	ant	

This page is intentionally left blank.

gl	ass	
gl	asses	
gl	obe	
gl	ad	
gl	ue	
gl	ove	
gl	ow	
gl	ide	

This page is intentionally left blank.

Resource: Cut and laminate to use as a resource.
Cut and match to complete the word and match
it with the correct picture.

bl	ue	
bl	ack	
bl	ade	
bl	ender	
bl	ocks	
bl	anket	
bl	oom	
bl	ood	

This page is intentionally left blank.

fl	ower	
fl	y	
fl	ask	
fl	ag	
fl	ock	
fl	oor	
fl	oat	
fl	amingo	

This page is intentionally left blank.

Resource: Cut and laminate to use as a resource.
Cut and match to complete the word and match
it with the correct picture.

br	ick	
br	own	
br	ead	
br	anch	
br	ain	
br	ide	
br	oom	
br	ush	

This page is intentionally left blank.

st	ick	
st	amp	
st	and	
st	ove	
st	one	
st	ore	
st	op	
st	ar	

This page is intentionally left blank.

Resource: Cut and laminate to use as a resource. Cut and match to complete the word and match it with the correct picture.

tr	ap	
tr	ain	
tr	ash	
tr	umpet	
tr	ack	
tr	unk	
tr	ee	
tr	uck	

This page is intentionally left blank.

Resource: Cut and laminate to use as a resource.
Cut and match to complete the word and match
it with the correct picture.

cr	y	
cr	ack	
cr	ib	
cr	ayon	
cr	ab	
cr	ane	
cr	oss	
cr	own	

This page is intentionally left blank.

The   **is**   **in**   **the**

tree   **ball**

---

to   **jog**   **not**   **run**

We   **like**

We   **went**   **by**   **the**

bike   **to**   **park**   **Sunday**

on

This page is intentionally left blank.

leaves	falling	are	to
ground	The	the	orange

is	a	tall	tree
This	oak		

I	to	play	baseball
in	the	park	like

This page is intentionally left blank.

on	Sam	is	going

swimming	Wednesday

She	dancing	was	the

drum	beat	to

likes	mathematics	He	but

language	hates	arts

This page is intentionally left blank.

asked	to	us	prepare
Teacher	The	quiz	for

They	playing	blocks	with
were			

Mary	playing	was	in
park	the		

This page is intentionally left blank.

Printed in Great Britain
by Amazon

81585721R00068